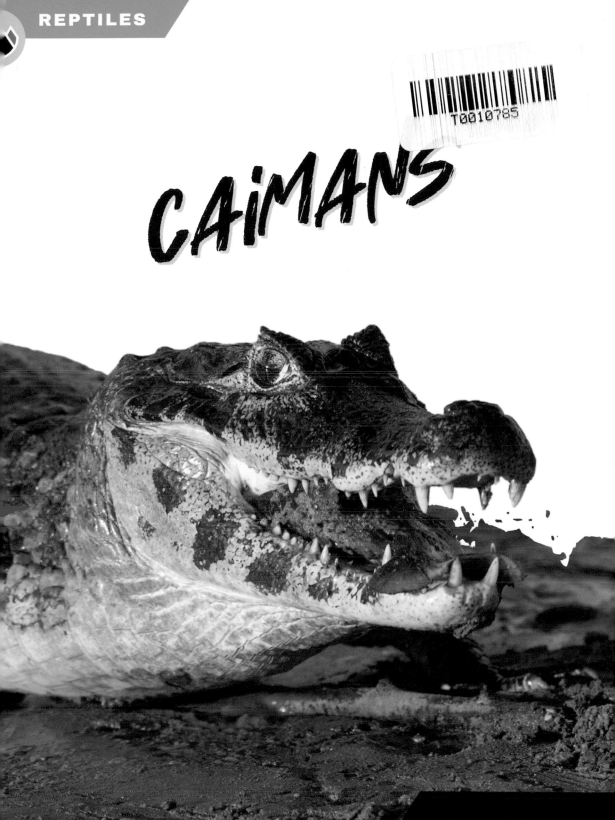

CAIMANS

BY JAMES BOW

Apex is distributed by North Star Editions:
sales@northstareditions.com | 888-417-0195

Produced for Apex by Red Line Editorial.

Photographs ©: Shutterstock Images, cover, 1, 4–5, 8–9, 10–11, 14, 15, 16–17, 18–19, 20, 22–23, 26, 29; Yoshiharu Sekino/Science Source, 6–7; iStockphoto, 12–13, 21, 27; Michel Gunther/Science Source, 24–25

Library of Congress Control Number: 2022920134

ISBN
978-1-63738-542-5 (hardcover)
978-1-63738-596-8 (paperback)
978-1-63738-701-6 (ebook pdf)
978-1-63738-650-7 (hosted ebook)

Printed in the United States of America
Mankato, MN
082023

NOTE TO PARENTS AND EDUCATORS

Apex books are designed to build literacy skills in striving readers. Exciting, high-interest content attracts and holds readers' attention. The text is carefully leveled to allow students to achieve success quickly. Additional features, such as bolded glossary words for difficult terms, help build comprehension.

TABLE OF CONTENTS

CHAPTER 1

PREDATOR AND PROTECTOR

A black caiman rests by a river. Her babies are nearby. She spots something move. An anaconda is swimming toward her.

Many caimans are found near slow-moving rivers.

Anacondas are large snakes. They can kill animals by squeezing.

The caiman waits until the anaconda gets close. Then she lunges. She bites the snake. It curls its body around her. But the caiman holds on.

CRUSHING BITE

Caimans have strong jaws. In fact, the black caiman has one of the strongest bites of all animals. Its jaws can easily break bones.

The caiman pulls the anaconda underwater. The anaconda lets go. So does the caiman. The snake rushes away. The caiman swims back to her babies. She kept them safe.

Caimans spend some of their time swimming and some time on land.

Caimans have long tails and short legs. That body shape makes them powerful swimmers.

CHAPTER 2

THE CAIMAN FAMILY

Caimans are **reptiles**. They look similar to alligators. But caimans are usually smaller. They don't have bones between their **nostrils**.

Like an alligator, a caiman's snout has a rounded shape.

Caimans live in South and
Central America. Many live in
rivers and swamps. But some
live in salt water.

WARM AND COOL

Caimans are **cold-blooded**. To stay warm, they lie in the sun. During hot times of year, they rest in burrows. This helps them stay cool.

Caimans sometimes rest on rocks or logs.

Black caimans can grow more than 15 feet (4.6 m) long.

There are six types of caimans. Black caimans are the largest. Cuvier's dwarf caimans are smallest. Other types are in the middle.

FAST FACT

Spectacled caimans have hard bumps between their eyes. The bumps look a bit like glasses.

Cuvier's dwarf caimans can grow up to 4 feet (1.2 m) long.

CHAPTER 3

HUNTING AND EATING

Caimans are **carnivores**. They hunt fish, insects, birds, and small animals. They can also be **scavengers**. They eat any food they can find.

Fish is a major part of most caimans' diets.

Caimans rest during the day. At night, they hunt. Their eyes and nostrils are on the top of their snouts. So, caimans can hide under the water. They can sneak up on **prey**.

A hiding caiman can look similar to a floating log.

FACING DANGER

Some people hunt caimans. People sell the skin and meat. Some species became **endangered** because of this. But new laws helped. The caimans aren't endangered anymore.

A caiman can swallow a fish in one bite.

Caimans move fast to catch prey. They grab the animals with their strong jaws. Caimans may also pull prey underwater to drown them.

Large caimans eat capybara. These furry animals live near rivers in South America.

CHAPTER 4

MAKING A NEST

Caimans usually live alone. But once a year, they look for **mates**. They rub backs, touch snouts, and blow bubbles. They do this to attract one another.

Caimans usually come together to mate between May and August.

After mating, female caimans build nests for eggs. They use leaves and plants. The eggs usually hatch 90 to 115 days later.

Many animals eat caiman eggs or newly hatched caimans.

HOT OR COLD

The temperature of a caiman's nest affects how the eggs hatch. Some nests are cooler. They hatch more females. Warmer nests hatch more males.

Catching prey can wear down caimans' teeth. But young and adult caimans can grow new teeth.

At first, the babies stay with their mothers. The babies learn to swim and find food. After 18 months, they can live alone.

FAST FACT

Most caimans live for about 30 to 40 years in the wild.

Caiman babies need extra care for a few months after hatching.

COMPREHENSION
QUESTIONS

Write your answers on a separate piece of paper.

1. Write a sentence describing how a caiman swims.

2. Would you want to meet a caiman in real life? Why or why not?

3. What type of caiman is the largest?

> **A.** spectacled caiman
>
> **B.** black caiman
>
> **C.** Cuvier's dwarf caiman

4. How could new laws help caimans no longer be endangered?

> **A.** The new laws could stop caimans from going near people.
>
> **B.** The new laws could get more people to hunt caimans.
>
> **C.** The new laws could stop people from hunting caimans.

5. What does **lunges** mean in this book?

The caiman waits until the anaconda gets close.
*Then she **lunges**. She bites the snake.*

    A. falls asleep

    B. moves quickly to attack

    C. runs away and hides

6. What does **burrows** mean in this book?

*During hot times of year, they rest in **burrows**.*
This helps them stay cool.

    A. hot desert areas

    B. large rocks in the sun

    C. holes in the ground

Answer key on page 32.

GLOSSARY

carnivores
Animals that eat meat.

cold-blooded
Having a body temperature that matches the temperature of the surrounding water or air.

endangered
In danger of dying out forever.

mates
Animals that come together to have babies.

nostrils
Openings in noses that animals can use for breathing and smelling.

prey
Animals that are hunted and eaten by other animals.

reptiles
Cold-blooded animals that have scales.

scavengers
Animals that eat dead animals they did not kill.

TO LEARN MORE

BOOKS

Downs, Kieran. *Giant Otter vs. Caiman*. Minneapolis: Bellwether Media, 2022.

Golkar, Golriz. *Crocodile*. Mendota Heights, MN: Apex Editions, 2023.

Ringstad, Arnold. *Totally Amazing Facts about Reptiles*. North Mankato, MN: Capstone Press, 2018.

ONLINE RESOURCES

Visit **www.apexeditions.com** to find links and resources related to this title.

ABOUT THE AUTHOR

James Bow writes novels and nonfiction children's books. He loves wild animals but knows to give them lots of space.

INDEX

ANSWER KEY:
1. Answers will vary; 2. Answers will vary; 3. B; 4. C; 5. B; 6. C